Skip·Beat!™
By Yoshiki Nakamura
Kyoko Mogami followed her true love Sho to Tokyo to support him while he made it big as an idol. But he's casting her out now that he's famous! Kyoko won't suffer in silence—she's going to get her sweet revenge by beating Sho in show biz!
Shojo Beat Manga
Skip·Beat!
Yoshiki Nakamura
1
Shojo Beat™
MANGA from the HEART
Only $8.99
On sale at:
www.shojobeat.com
viz

library wars

Volume 6
Shojo Beat Edition

Story & Art by **Kiiro Yumi**
Original Concept by **Hiro Arikawa**

ENGLISH TRANSLATION Kinami Watabe
ADAPTATION & LETTERING Sean McCoy
DESIGN Amy Martin
EDITOR Megan Bates

Printed in the U.S.A.

Published by VIZ Media, LLC
P.O. Box 77010
San Francisco, CA 94107

10 9 8 7 6 5 4 3 2 1
First printing, September 2011

www.shojobeat.com www.viz.com

Kiiro Yumi won the 42nd *LaL*
Manga Grand Prix Fresh Debu
award for her manga *Billy*
Bocchan no Yuutsu (Little Bill
Depression). Her latest serie
is *Toshokan Senso Love&Wa*
(Library Wars: Love & War)
which runs in *LaLa* magazin
in Japan and is published in
English by VIZ Media.

Hiro Arikawa won the 10th
Dengeki Novel Prize for her
work *Shio no Machi: Wish on M*
Precious in 2003 and debutec
with the same novel in 2004.
Of her many works, Arikawa i
best known for the *Library Wa*
series and her *Jieitai Sanbusak*
trilogy, which consists of *Sor*
no Naka (In the Sky), *Umi nc*
Soko (The Bottom of the Sea
and *Shio no Machi* (City of Sal

End notes

Page 10, panel 2: Valentine's Day
In Japan Valentine's Day is an opportunity for women to show their romantic interests by giving chocolate to the guys they're interested in.

Page 13, panel 5: Achoo
In Japan it's thought that people sneeze when someone's talking about them behind their backs.

Page 14, panel 1: Courtesy Chocolate
In Japanese, *giri-choco*. Some women also give their colleagues chocolates on Valentine's Day, and it's considered a (nonromantic) seasonal gift.

Page 112, panel 2: Norakuro
Norakuro, a black and white soldier-dog, is the main character of the manga of the same name.

Page 128, panel 1: Suplex
Suplex is a kind of offensive move used in professional wrestling: the wrestler picks up the opponent and then uses his or her own body weight to drive them back down onto the mat.

My sister, a mother of three, was happy with it.

Special Thanks!!

Ms. Arikawa
Ms. Arikawa's editor (ASCII Media)

★

Mamada, Murakami,
Aoki, Asahina

★

My family

★

My editor

★

Everyone who makes this series possible.

★★

Thank you for supporting me!

Hope to see you in the next volume.

Kiiro Yumi

弓きいろ

WHAT ...?!
WHAT ARE YOU ...!
YELLING STUFF LIKE THAT...!
What's this?
SIR... DID YOU JUST BLUSH?
NO, I DID NOT!
He blushed. Hooray!
Shut up, you shameless wench!
WHAT'S THAT ABOUT?
KIDS...
THE END

EXTRA BONUS MANGA 3
SORRY ABOUT THAT.
GOOD JOB, KASAHARA. THERE'S NO NEED TO APOLOGIZE. GO TO BED. DISMISSED!
FWIP
...
Instructor Dojo is calm and in control.
Here I am in my yukata, all excited and worked up over what just happened.
Nothing seems to faze him.
YOU REALLY DO HAVE AN EXCELLENT BODY, SIR!
Harassment.

EXTRA BONUS MANGA 2
The police took them away.
Mission accomplished.
SALUTE
GOOD NIGHT.
NIGHT NIGHT.
YAWN
...
I'M SO SORRY...
I WAS STUPID...! I REPENT! I REPENT!
HAHAHA
boil bubble
I SWEAR IT WON'T HAPPEN AGAIN!
WE'LL BE MODEL PRISONERS...!
I THOUGHT YOU TURNED IN.
I TRIED TO.
BEER
VENDING MACHINE

EXTRA BONUS MANGA 1
What's Moburo doing, you ask?
TNK TNK
Hot spring...
Kasahara is around somewhere.
The tension builds during our romantic getaway.
Technically *not* a romantic getaway.
Hey, Moburo!
Let's play ping-pong, okay?
My heart thumps at the sight of her in a yukata, trembles to see her after a nice hot soak.
This trip will bring us closer than ever...
Just imagining. Heh heh.
KLAK
You have an excellent body, sir.
Block-head.
THAT'S IT, MAN, GAME OVER, MAN, GAME OVER!

BONUS MANGA / THE END

You...
YOU HAVE AN EXCELLENT BODY, SIR.
BONG
BLOCK-HEAD!
Get off.
Today was not my lucky day...
So...
BLUP

...
OH...
SPIN SPIN
AH...

SPLASH

Reflex.
UGH!
UH...
SLIP
AWE-SOME!
HEY!

A MEN'S ONLY HOT SPRING!
HA HA! COME IN IF YOU DARE!
KRAK KRAK
NO SWEAT
NOOOO!
SIR, THEY'RE THE BANK ROBBERS!
CATCH THEM!

THANKS.
OOPS.
WHAT?
I WAS TOO DROWSY TO HOLD BACK...
WOW!
Is he dead?!
FREEEEEEEZE!
I DON'T WANNA!
What a fast runner! There's no time for me to wallow in self-pity.
MEN
Damn.
NOW HOW ABOUT THIS...?
KRAK

THUD
UGH
TEZU-
KA...

TWO AGAINST ONE. KASAHARA NEEDS BACKUP.
TEXTS SENT TO ALL THREE...
But...
INSTRUCTOR DOJO IS IN THE BATH.
SNEAK
...
UHH. BOSS TOLD ME TO RUN, BUT...
I CAN'T LET IT PASS!
YOU WICKED TEMPTRESS WITH A FACE LIKE AN ANGEL...
...YOU STEPPED ON HIS HEART AND BROKE IT!

ARE THESE ALL MADE OF GLASS?
THAT'S RIGHT. CUTE, HUH?
IT'S HANDMADE.
THEY'RE VERY POPULAR WITH YOUNG WOMEN.
GIFT SHOP
I'LL TAKE ONE...
BUMP
SHATTER

WAAAAH
RUN FOR YOUR LIFE!
DA
SH!!
BOSS!
KASA-HARA.
LEAVE IT TO ME!
TMP TMP TMP TMP TMP
Noisy.
...

from: Hikaru Tezuka
Bingo.
I found wads of money in their room.
BEEP
I WAS RIGHT!
GASP!
GUILTY AS...
MASARU.
wheeze...

Oops.
I LEFT THE KEY ON THE PING-PONG TABLE.
WHAT?!
WHAT'S YOUR PROBLEM, DUMMY!
GO GET IT!
BANK ROBBERS?
YEP.
THE MOMENT I LAID MY EYES ON THEM...
A STRIKING RESEM-BLANCE TO THE ROBBERS CAUGHT ON CAMERA.
Caught on Camera
BLURRY
It's too blurry to tell!
Sharp eyes!
TEZUKA EXPLAINED IT TO THE OWNER AND HE'S CHECKING THEIR ROOM AS WE SPEAK.
OH. GOT A TEXT.

THANKS FOR THE GOOD TIME, GUYS!
WE WORKED UP QUITE A SWEAT. WE'LL TAKE ANOTHER DIP IN THE HOT SPRING AND CALL IT A NIGHT!
G'night!
BURNED
(tired from losing)
Shiba-zaki invited them along?
That's...
HMM... ANOTHER BATH SOUNDS GOOD.
Sweaty.
I'LL BE IN THE SOUVENIR SHOP.
PLIK
Boss!
HANG ON, BOSS.
Uhh. Shibazaki... My lucky day has ended in disaster.
DRAG DRAG
...
OH!
...hard to believe.

HEEZ
HEEZ
HEEZ
DA...
DAMN YOU.
10 GAMES TOTAL DEFEAT
BAM BAM BAM BAM BAM
IT'S NOT YOU, KASAHARA.
I'M JUST TOO STRONG.
YOU'RE GOING TO PAY.
GRIN
EH?
SOME NEW FACES.
And Tezuka's gone.
YEAH. I SAW THEM IN THE BATH. THEY'RE ALSO GUESTS.
SHIBAZAKI INVITED THEM TO JOIN US.
WHOA! YOU COULD SEE ALL THAT DURING THE GAME...?!
HUMPH
OF COURSE.
Hold on.

Five minutes later
BOSS!
YOU LOSE
I couldn't see the ball.
HA HA HA
Don't give up.
Okay, one more time!
WHAT'S UP, DROWSY?
I've never seen you like this.
I WAS READING A MYSTERY NOVEL BEFORE I WENT TO BED. ONCE I STARTED, I COULDN'T PUT IT DOWN.
YAWN
I WAS COUNTING ON GRABBING A NAP IN THE CAR.
No such luck.
The bad seat...
Superior officers right and left.
SORRY, SLEEPY-HEAD, BUT I NEED YOUR HELP...
HUH?

You can do it, Kasahara.
WOULD YOU LIKE TO JOIN US OR ARE YOU HAPPY OVER HERE?
Oh.
Um.
Trying to forever etch the sight of Shibazaki into their memories.
Please, don't mind...
...us.
The more the merrier...
Right? ♡
DON'T GET INVOLVED!
SSSH
SSSH
SSSH
TWO MORE PARTICIPANTS.
OH, HELLO.
LET'S USE THE ONE IN THE BACK.
The other table is going to be occupied for a long time.
Today is my day!
You go, boss!
WATCH ME, SHIBAZAKI!
Win the game and her heart!

6

*

This is the last one.

Thanks so much for reading this far.

I had a lot of fun working on the volume.

The more I draw, the more I feel attached to these characters. Isn't it great?

Thank you for your continued support of the series.

Bye-bye! Please read the Special Thanks at the end of the book.

Kiiro Yumi

弓きいろ

*

*

This is fun!
It's like...
...a night on a school trip.
SO MUCH PASSION AND ENERGY...
YAAAAHH!
PING PONG PING PONG PING PONG
...LIKE TWO EXCITABLE HIGH SCHOOL BOYS.
I know!

DON'T GET INVOLVED ...!
Oh, dear.
All freshened up and in a yukata...!
Hey.
YOU WANTED TO PLAY PING-PONG, RIGHT?
WHERE'S THE TABLE?
OH.
OVER HERE.

THERE ARE YOUNG PEOPLE HERE.
Did you see their abs?
DON'T BE SCARED, MASARU!
TODAY'S OUR LUCKY DAY. WE'LL BE FINE AS LONG AS WE KEEP A LOW PROFILE.
pip pop
IF YOU SEE A PRETTY GIRL, IGNORE HER AND LAY LOW.
Zzz Zzz
An excep-tion to the rule!
GASP
...
GRIN
B-BMP
B-BMP
DON'T...

I SAW A PING-PONG TABLE.
WHAT DO YOU SAY TO A MATCH AFTER THE BATH?
SOUNDS LIKE A PLAN.
YOU IN, DOJO?
YEP.
ZZZ
GLARE
BOW
Hello there.
BOW
...
LET'S GET OUT.
Yeah.
Wake up, Tezuka.
Uh-huh.
HEY, BOSS.

SPLASH
ZZZ ZZZ
ARE YOU STILL IN THERE?
Oh, Instructor Komaki.
Yes, sir. It feels surreal.
YES, IT SURE DOES.

IN THE SLOW SEASON, IT'S NOT SUCH A BAD THING FOR THE INN.
We have footage of the robbers.
THIS MONTH'S BEEN CRAZY... WHY NOT UNWIND A BIT...
ZZZ
ZZZ
...EVERY ONCE IN A WHILE?
THE TWO BANK ROBBERS MADE OFF WITH 20 MILLION YEN. THEY ARE STILL ON THE LOOSE.
YEAH.
THE POLICE ARE TRYING TO TRACK DOWN THE SUSPECTS.

Great view!
Excel-lent dinner!
Back from dinner to find the perfectly made futon.
Top-notch service!
All kinds of swag.
Happy♥
LIVING THE GOOD LIFE FOR THE FIRST TIME, EH?
LET'S CHECK OUT THE HOT SPRING.
Dinner was great!
Were there other female librarians?
Middle-aged ones, yes. It's more fun to be with you guys.
BUT... ISN'T THIS A BIT *TOO* GOOD?
Next up...
Well... THE OWNER OF THIS INN IS FRIENDS WITH THE HEAD LIBRARIAN.
I UNDER-STAND THEY GAVE US A GOOD DISCOUNT.

5

*

Tezuka's big brother appeared for the first time in the final chapter of the volume.

He's going to be quite a busy man in the series. I'm already a fan! (*laughs*) He's very different from the characters I usually draw for my original stories. It's fun and refreshing and educational. You're a very educational character, big brother!

Drawing his glasses is a lot of work, though... I hate it when they end up crooked...

*

*

THERE'S A HOT SPRING IN THE NEIGHBOR-HOOD?
Hello, this is Iku Kasahara.
yippee!
Today we're visiting a library outside of Tokyo to help prepare for their remodel.
Countryside
The Task Force helped move books and clean up while a few librarians provided referencing guidance.
Sweet.
I BOOKED A NICE HOTEL FOR YOU. THANKS FOR COMING ALL THIS WAY, EVERYONE.
Head Librarian
YES, THERE IS. FURTHER UP THE MOUNTAIN.
A VERY NICE HOT SPRING.
OH, BOY!
Shibazaki, too.
It looks like...
Sweet.

CAW
CAW
A hot spring?
THIS TIME OF YEAR IT'S JUST GONNA BE A BUNCH OF OLD GEEZERS.
NOTHING TO BE SCARED OF.
YOU'RE SO COOL, BOSS!

WE'RE NOW DEEP ENOUGH INTO THE WOODS.
YEAH.
IT WENT WELL. WE'RE IN LUCK TODAY!
HEY.
DOINAKA INN
FSHHHH
THE TANK IS EMPTY!
In the middle of nowhere.
OH, NO. WHAT SHOULD WE DO?
LOOK!
A HOT SPRING?
HOT SPRING
NEXT EXIT
DOINAKA INN
GREAT. LET'S SPEND THE NIGHT HERE. I'M HUNGRY ANYWAY.
They'll help us get some gas.
But there'll be a lot of people in the hotel... What if someone sees us and—
SLAM
IDIOT.

BONUS MANGA

Privileged.

He's just being honest.

LIBRARY WARS LOVE & WAR VOL 6/THE END

ENLISTED INTO THE TASK FORCE AT THE TOP OF HIS CLASS.
A TOP-NOTCH SHOOTER IN THE FIELD AND SELECTED AS A SNIPER. HAS SHOWN EXCELLENT DESKWORK SKILLS.
THE LIBRARY'S NEW STAR, RECOGNIZED AS SUCH BY SUPERIOR OFFICERS AND NEW RECRUITS.
SHIF
...OUT-STANDING.
HE'S INDEED MY BROTHER.

FLOOF
You're smart. I'm proud of you.
When you grow up, we'll work together and fight for libraries.
Hikaru.

IT'S NICE TO HAVE BROTHERS.
AS LONG AS THEY DON'T CAUSE TROUBLE.
ONE MINUTE LEFT.
Better dash.
Oh, gosh.
Bro.
Look. I solved all these problems.
You got all of them right.

NEXT TIME YOU FIGHT, DO IT SOMEWHERE LESS DANGEROUS, OKAY?
IS THAT THE BEST ADVICE YOU CAN MUSTER?
THANKS, EVIL LADY.
Bye.
IDIOT! SHE'S NOT EVIL.
DON'T YOU KNOW WHO THEY ARE?
THE KANTO LIBRARY FORCES.
THEY'RE HEROES.

...BASING THAT ON WHAT, YOU RECKLESS MORON?!
...
BUT I WAS RIGHT. I DID GOOD.
ADMIT IT.
...
BONG
WHY THE FIST ?!
She fell down...
WHISPER
WHISPER
She fell down and is laughing...
WHISPER
THANKS SO MUCH.

...him.
Right?
HEH HEH HEH.
I KNEW IT.
I KNEW YOU'D SAVE ME.
SIR!
AND YOU ARE...

Sometimes you get it from your brothers... Sometimes from your colleagues.
Like...

CORPORAL KASAHARA...
WHOOSH
Trust.

DASH
SQUIRT
WAIT, GINGA. I'M NOT MAD ANYMORE!
WHAT?
TRIP
WHIP
GIN-

...made me who I am today.
GINGA!
CRINGE
SQUIRT
CORPORAL KASAHARA! UP THERE...
ON THE FOOT-BRIDGE!
hff hff
TAIGA ...!
...and the evil lady.

Stupid Iku!
Dumb Iku!
Nasty tongues, quick with fists. They could be mean, believe me...
But...
When I was in a fix, they always came to my rescue.
BIG BRO!
That's trust. That's love.
And I believe *that*...

OH MY GOD, CORPORAL KASAHARA...
I...
SLAP
RELAX!
UGH!
YOU'VE GOT THE KANTO LIBRARY FORCE TO BACK YOU UP!
I used to wander off...
GINGA!
GINGA!
...when I was playing with my brothers in the mountains.

BY THE WAY...
I DON'T THINK YOUR BROTHER WANTED THE GUN FOR HIMSELF.
hff
hff
HE LAID OUT EVERY BIT OF MONEY HE HAD AND TOLD ME THAT IT WAS FOR TAIGA. ALL WITH A HAPPY LOOK ON HIS FACE.
OH...
HA HA
GO EASY ON THAT LITTLE THING.
DASH
DAMN ...!
GINGA!
ANY LUCK?
NO...
WE CHECKED THE STREET THOR-OUGHLY.

DASH
OH...
TAIGA.
ARE YOU SURE...
...THIS IS WHAT YOU WANT?
GRIT
HMM? THAT LITTLE BOY?
I HAVEN'T SEEN HIM...
TOYS

GRAB
EEK!
WHERE DID YOU LAST SEE HIM?!
IN F-FRONT OF THE T-TOY STORE.
CORPORAL KASAHARA!
TEN MINUTES UNTIL WORK.
FIND HIM BY THEN, TEZUKA.
YES, SIR.

TAIGA?
OH. HELLO AGAIN.
BOW
ON YOUR OWN? WHERE'S YOUR BROTHER?
I DON'T CARE.
OH?
...
WHAT HAPPENED? YOU HAD A FIGHT?
Wait.
DON'T TELL ME YOU...
YOU LEFT YOUR BROTHER ALONE SOME-WHERE?
VROOM
HONK

HOW MANY TIMES DO I HAVE TO APOLOGIZE FOR YOU IN ONE DAY...?
IF YOU KEEP DOING THIS TO ME, I'LL NEVER HANG OUT WITH YOU AGAIN...
THE HELL WITH YOU!
Thank you, sir!
That was the loveliest meal ever!
THAT WAS MONEY WELL SPENT, SEEING HOW HAPPY IT MADE YOU. RIGHT, DOJO?
...
Maybe.
HMM?

IS THAT SQUIRT GUN COOL OR WHAT?
I KNEW YOU'D-
SLAP
PLOK
ROLL ROLL
KNOCK IT OFF...!

HEY!
I'M SO SORRY.
WELL, HE'S JUST A KID. I'LL LET IT SLIDE.
ARE YOU HIS BIG BROTHER?
YOU SHOULD KEEP AN EYE ON HIM, OKAY?
TAIGA.
Taiga paid for it.
SQUIRT

SQUIRT GUN GUN
Spray Distance 8m
Hi.
YOU LIKE THAT SQUIRT-GUN, HMM?
STARE
WHERE'S YOUR MOM AND DAD?
Taiga always says...
THE LIBRARY FORCES ARE SO COOL. I WANT TO BE LIKE THEM!
WOW!
PRESENT
AWESOME. LIKE A REAL LIBRARY AGENT.
THANKS, GINGA!
I'LL BUY IT.
all his money
plink
Hmm...
That's not enough, kid.
THIS IS FOR TAIGA.

...
I...
HERE WE ARE.
ENJOY YOUR APPETIZERS.
TNK
Ohmigod.
THIS IS AMAZING!
Nothing like my normal lunch.
KEEP YOUR VOICE DOWN. YOU'RE EMBARRASSING US.
I'M SO GLAD I ORDERED THE MOST EXPENSIVE THING.
I DON'T KNOW WHERE TO BEGIN...
glee
SIGH
Thank you, sir.
TOY SHOP

WHEN WE FOUGHT, WE WENT ALL-OUT.
Brother
IT WOULD QUICKLY GO FROM A SQUABBLE TO A HAND-TO-HAND SCUFFLE TO A SERIES OF SUPLEX THROWS.
Sweet memories...
Grown up and still wrestling.
YOU HAVE A LITTLE SISTER, INSTRUCTOR DOJO?
WAS A SUPLEX *YOUR* FAVORITE MOVE?
Nah.
WRESTLING WASN'T MY METHOD OF RESOLVING A FAMILY QUARREL.
Thanks for giving me a glimpse into your twisted roots.
Are you ridi-culing me?
Heh
I'm an only child. Sounds like fun, though.
HOW ABOUT YOU, TEZUKA?
ANY BROTHERS OR SISTERS?

4

*

My room is so messy. Things go missing all the time...

Right in front of me one minute, gone the next. I call it *illusion.* While working on this volume, *illusion* struck and I lost a very important item. It really bummed me out... Oh, well...

Luckily, there was a *substitute...* My fear is that one day I might lose something that is not replaceable.

SIGH

When will I learn...?

*

*

I'M SO SORRY. DID MY BROTHER BOTHER YOU?
GINGA! WHAT DID I TELL YOU ABOUT USING THAT SQUIRT GUN?!
BOP
Evil...
OH, NO. DON'T WORRY ABOUT ME.
Cute Kid.
Wait.
YOU'RE...
OH.
TAIGA ?!
AAAAHH
CORPORAL KASA-HARA!
Taiga Yoshikawa. He starts high school next year.
He first appeared in Chapters 10-11! Refer to Volume 3!
Wow. Long time no see!
It's so nice to see you!
SO THIS IS YOUR LITTLE BROTHER, HUH?
Spittin' image.
HE'S A BIT OF A HANDFUL.
HE WANDERS OFF THE SECOND I LOOK AWAY.
This big woman is evil, Taiga.
Shut up!
BOP

I'M A LIBRARY AGENT.
EVIL LADY!
SPURT
...
SPURT
EVIL LADY!
THAT KID IGNORED THE KING OF CRANKY AND ATTACKED KASAHARA.
YAY YAY
You got me.
SHE MUST HAVE HAD A REALLY EVIL LOOK ON HER FACE.
Barrier
HEY, GINGA!

ARE YOU TREATING THE ENTIRE TEAM, BOSS?
DON'T PUSH IT, KOMAKI.
JUST KASA-HARA AND TEZUKA.
VROOM
YOU ARE TREATING ME AS WELL, SIR?
THERE'S NO NEED TO BE MODEST.
SPURT
HOW ABOUT WE BOTH ORDER THE MOST EXPENSIVE STUFF ON THE MENU...?
I GOT YOU, EVIL LADY!

DO YOU HAVE A PROBLEM WITH THAT, SIR?
A man's word is his bond.
AREN'T YOU CLEVER, PICKING A FANCY RESTAU-RANT.
NOW, NOW. WE DID HAVE A LAUGH AT HER EXPENSE.
WE OWE THIS TO HER.
Mainly you...
YOU'RE COMING TOO, TEZUKA.
Lunch.
YES, SIR.
We're gradu-ally getting over the shock...
...caused by Weekly New World.

Ten days have passed since the Norakuro Face incident.
SORRY ABOUT THAT. I'LL BUY YOU LUNCH.
The bruise is gone.
I VOTE FOR THE FRENCH RESTAURANT BY THE BUS DEPOT.

5.
GOOOOAL!!
We figured as much.
GALLERY

CHAPTER 28

WELL, HE HAD A POINT, AND...
NOBODY HAS TO KNOW ABOUT US IF WE EMAIL EACH OTHER.
I see!
I HOPE THEY WON'T BUG YOU ANYMORE.
I know you hate the spotlight.
Tell me what made you decide to exchange email addresses with him!
GRIN
It was you, Kasahara.
FLICK
Not...
...a...
...word. ♡
GWAH!
Well, you wouldn't get it if I told you.
NO, NO, NO. NOT MY FACE, SHIBAZAKI!

...really...
Wow.
YOU GAVE HIM YOUR EMAIL ADDRESS?

WHAT YOU JUST SAID... THAT'S NOT A GOOD ENOUGH REASON!
IF YOU WANT TO TURN ME DOWN, FIND REAL FAULTS IN ME!
He's really...
Wow.

YOU'RE RIGHT. I FIRST NOTICED YOU BECAUSE I LIKE THE WAY YOU LOOK.
BUT.
THE MOMENT YOU OPENED YOUR MOUTH, I COULD TELL YOU ARE MERCILESSLY SARCASTIC.
MURMUR
MURMUR
AND THAT'S THE PART OF YOU I WANTED TO KNOW BETTER! THEREFORE...

GOOD DAY.
TMP
A man so honest and open like Kasahara... He deserves to see the real me.
You won't see it this way now, but...
I'm doing this because I respect you.
WAIT A MINUTE!

CLIK
REPLY
I know.
CLIK
So...
Here I go.
THE POINT IS, MEN WHO CAN'T SEE BEYOND MY LOOKS...
...ARE NOT WELCOME.
THERE YOU HAVE IT.
TMP

...
NOTHING.
?
Kasa-hara. You always make everyone feel better...
Ha!
...without even knowing it.
I'm laughing myself to death...
This is killing me...
*Komaki
BEEP
E-mail
From Ryusuke Genda
no subject
Sorry.

I THOUGHT YOU'D ALL BE HANGING YOUR HEADS. ESPECIALLY CHIEF GENDA.
Package for you.
Thanks.
I KNOW.
Are you still laughing?!!
Nora-kuro...
KASAHARA'S FACE IS JUST WHAT THIS PLACE NEEDED.
Sorry about that. I'll buy you lunch.
Look me in the eye when you talk.
SHE HAS A TALENT FOR TURNING COINCIDENCE INTO LAUGHTER.
BY THE WAY, SHIBAZAKI. ABOUT THAT GUY...
HM?

WHAT THE...
WHAT'S UP WITH YOU, LOOKING LIKE NORAKURO?! GET ONE FOR THE RIGHT EYE TO MATCH!
NO-NO-NORA-KURO?!
AH HA HA HA HA HA HA!
For crying out loud, knock it off.
WAAH
WAAH
FUME
OH, MY. LOOKS LIKE I'M A LITTLE LATE FOR THE PARTY.
Norakuro
A manga from before the war. Everyone's familiar with it because the library has the series.

YOU SHOULD BE HONORED TO BE WOUNDED IN THE LINE OF DUTY.
Yesterday
Morning Shiner
SHOULDN'T BLAME YOU? YOU'RE MY BOSS! ACT LIKE IT!
SPURT
GOOD MORNING...
AHA HA HA
HA HA HA HA HA HA HA HA
No way.
Stop it, Komaki. You're making it worse.
HA HA
...
BAM
I'M GOING TO SUE YOU ALL FOR ABUSE OF AUTHORITY!
WHAT'S THE COMMO- TION!
CHIEF...

SPURT
WHA-?
NGH.
CAN YOU BLAME ME? TAKE A LOOK IN THE MIRROR.
WHAT WAS THAT FOR?
Spitting in a girl's face?
GASP
IMAGINE GETTING CORNERED BY A FACE LIKE THAT. YOU LOOK HILARIOUS.
SNICKER
I was trying to avert my gaze.

WHAT ABOUT THE CHIEF ...?
EVEN IF THE CHIEF SPEAKS UP AGAINST COMMANDER INAMINE...
...HE DOESN'T HAVE THE AUTHORITY TO SUPPORT HIS OPINION.
CHIEF
IS IT POSSIBLE THAT ETO LED US ON?!
I'VE HEARD HE'S REALLY GOOD.

The news came this morning.
WEEKLY NEW WORLD IS BANNED?!
THAT'S THE CONCLUSION THE MUSASHINO LIBRARY ARRIVED AT?!
BUT... WHY?
BANNED? NOT RESTRICTED ACCESS?!
ACCORDING TO THE LIBRARIANS...
...ETO'S OPINION CARRIED A LOT OF WEIGHT.
I WOULD LIKE YOU TO LOOK AT THESE ISSUES WITH A BROADER VISION AND BALANCE.
WE'LL COPY THE OTHER ARTICLES AND PUT THEM OUT WITH THE NEXT ISSUE. THAT'S THE BEST WE CAN DO.

BEING NICE IS PART OF MY JOB.
••••• WHAT? ••
This is a bit *too* direct.
I must spend too much time with that straight shooter.
4.

WELL, I DON'T BLAME YOU. A PRETTY GIRL SMILES AT YOU AND YOU FALL FOR HER. SIMPLE AS THAT.
CHAPTER 27

CHAPTER 27
WOULD YOU STOP DOING THIS? ASKING ME OUT FOR LUNCH?
IS THIS ABOUT WHAT HAPPENED YESTERDAY?
She definitely likes you.
YOU THINK I'D LET IT GO TO MY HEAD?
NO, IT'S NOT YOU.
BUT, YEAH. I'D HATE TO GIVE HER THE SATISFACTION BY HOOKING UP WITH YOU.
I HATE TO BREAK IT TO YOU, BUT...
THE GIRL YOU ARE INTERESTED IN... THE SOFT-SPOKEN, MILD-MANNERED LIBRARIAN... THAT'S NOT ME.

He's Normally a Smart Guy.

DON'T MAKE HIM WORRY. HE'LL GO BALD BECAUSE OF YOU.
HE WASN'T WORRIED ABOUT ME!
Just another excuse to yell at me.
NOW THAT'S WHAT I CALL BEING UNGRATEFUL.
WHAT ARE YOU TALKING ABOUT?!
I like you...
And it looks like the abusive instructor shares my sentiments.

What a handful!
You ungrateful little girl.
SHOCK
WHAT?!
Me?!

HE DID?
DAMN RIGHT! HE STARTED YELLING AT ME THE SECOND HE WALKED INTO THE HOSPITAL.
sip
EMERGENCY SERVICES WHITE FOUNTAIN HOSPITAL
YOU BLOCK-HEAD!
EEK!
I DID MY JOB. I COULD USE AN ENCOURAGING WORD.
That's all I ever wanted...
RUNNING INTO THE DOOR? THATS LAME EVEN BY SLAPSTICK COMEDY STANDARDS.
GRIND GRIND GRIND GRIND
DO YOU EVER TIRE OF ABUSING YOUR ALREADY DAMAGED HEAD?
GRIND
GRIND
It hurts, sir.
GRIND
Damn.

This is why I like you...
...Kasahara.
I WAS ABOUT TO ENTER THE BUILDING, CARRYING THE LATEST ISSUE OF WEEKLY NEW WORLD...
BUT THE AUTOMATIC DOOR WASN'T FULLY OPEN, AND...
YOU RAN INTO THE DOOR?!
THAT'S SO IDIOTIC!
AH HA HA HA HA HA HA!!!
This stupidity is legendary.
WELL, I'M GLAD TO HEAR...
...IT'S NOT AS BAD AS IT LOOKS.
THEY LAUGHED AT ME.
SNIFFLE
INSTRUCTOR DOJO WENT BERSERK.

And there you go.
You've done it.

IT DOESN'T MATTER IF HE'S A GOOD CATCH! IT'S SHIBAZAKI'S CHOICE TO MAKE!
WHAT HAPPENED TO YOUR FACE?
POINT
MY FACE IS NOT THE ISSUE HERE.
IT IS NOW.
THIS IS ABOUT SHIBA-ZAKI.
...
Don't glare at me! Your face is too painful to look at!
What?
FUME
FUME

STOP IT ALREADY!
EVEN IF HE'S A NICE PERSON... YOU'RE ONLY PUSHING HER AWAY FROM HIM!
BZZT BZZT BZZT
IT DOESN'T MATTER...
Wait a minute.
Kasahara?

Do it.
Why is Shiba-zaki...
...so arro-gant?
And go back to that lonely place.
BANG

Maybe he's going to bring it to another level. ♡
IT'S NOT WHAT YOU THINK. I'M JUST HELPING WITH HIS RESEARCH.
Come on! That's just the setup for a romantic moment!
Stop.
He's a handsome man! What's stopping you, hmm?
Go for it!
I just want to be left alone.
WHAT'S STOPPING ME...?
And he seems so sweet! ♡ ♡
Don't be manipulated. Can't you see what she's trying to do here?
First of all, you're too pretty to be single.
This is irritat-ing.
She's right. You need a boyfriend.
WHY WOULD I GO OUT WITH SOMEONE I DON'T EVEN LIKE? WHO I DATE IS NONE OF YOUR BUSINESS.
Say it.
You've done it before.

Why do I have to be humiliated just because your heart-throb has a crush on me?
CAFETERIA
Hey.
Are you two still on for lunch tomorrow?!
YAY
EXCUSE ME...?
SORRY, I COULDN'T HELP BUT OVER-HEAR.
MR. ASAHINA LIKES YOU, SHIBAZAKI.
Ohmigod!

GASP
She's waiting for you to take action, you know.
OH...
TMP
I know Hirose's plan.
TMP
TMP
Oh! It's Miss Shibazaki.
It's the usual.
Hirose
Wants to get a rival out of the game.
Librarian A
Shibazaki
Why?

She definitely likes you.
Um...
Okay...
THE PROBLEM IS SHE CAN'T TAKE THE INITIATIVE.
YOU HAVE TO *PUSH* HER.
You're the man here.
...
Hirose!

Always the straight shooter.
HOW ABOUT LUNCH TOMORROW?
Where would you like to go?
I'm fine with the same café.
TMP TMP
WOMEN
FLUSH
Shibazaki is too shy to let it show, but...
...This is her we're talking about.

Issue 15 of Weekly New World Not Available Until Further Notice
IT'S QUITE A HOT TOPIC, HUH.
I SUPPOSE.
DO YOU MIND IF I ASK YOU WHAT *YOUR* OPINION IS?
Ooh. Worker bee, aren't you?
SMILE
How admirable.
OH.
WELL.
SCRATCH
ACTUALLY, I'M JUST TRYING TO ASK YOU OUT.
I WAS WONDERING, MAYBE LUNCH TOGETHER?
...
I knew you were asking me out, silly. I was just teasing you.

MURMUR
MURMUR
THERE'S BEEN TOO MUCH FOCUS ON PRINCIPLES.
I UNDERSTAND THERE ARE TWO OPPOSING PHILOSOPHICAL CAMPS HERE. BUT WE'RE ONE IN THE SAME ORGANIZATION. WE FIGHT SIDE BY SIDE, NOT AGAINST EACH OTHER.
I WOULD LIKE YOU TO LOOK AT THESE ISSUES WITH A BROADER VISION AND BALANCE.
"Balance."
I see.
No personal agenda. Neutral and fair.
That's how Mr. Eto operates.
HELLO.

I THINK...
...NO ONE HAS YET MENTIONED THE POSSIBILITY OF BANNING THIS MONTH'S ISSUE.
?!
BUT THAT WOULD DENY ACCESS TO OTHER ARTICLES.
THAT'S NOT OUR POLICY.
THE MOST IMPORTANT THING IS KEEPING OUR AUTONOMY.
SOME, IF NOT MANY, OTHER LIBRARIES CONDONE THIS SORT OF BAN.
IT IS FOOLISH TO COMPLETELY EXCLUDE IT AS AN OPTION FOR CONSIDER-ATION.
I SEE WHY WE ARE CRITICIZED FOR BEING BIASED AND ONE-SIDED.

I THINK IT'D BE UNWISE TO CUT OR BLACK OUT PAGES.
IT'LL PREVENT US FROM EVENTUALLY RELEASING THE MATERIAL.
AND NO TAPING OVER THE ARTICLE. ANYONE CAN PEEL IT OFF AND READ IT.
HOW ABOUT WE MAKE A COPY OF THE ARTICLE, REDACT IT NOW, AND THEN REPLACE IT AT A LATER DATE?
By giving young agents an opportunity to speak, he encourages us to participate.
Everyone's so focused. Feeling energy in the room is a nice change.
As opposed to Toba's meetings:
DROWSY
He's good...
But...
WHAT'S YOUR TAKE ON IT?
He hasn't yet voiced his opinion.
LIEUTENANT COLONEL HATANO DEPUTY LIBRARIAN

BAM
KASA-
HARA!

THEY'RE HERE.
RUN!
SWISH
RUN, KASAHARA! MAKE IT TO THE BUILDING!
ROGER!

TMP
TCH
General Sadahiko Eto is the new head.
This is his first crisis conference.
THANKS FOR COMING, EVERY-ONE.
SHALL WE BEGIN?
Let's see what you're made of.
REGARDING ACCESS TO THE LATEST ISSUE OF *WEEKLY NEW WORLD*...
FIRST, I WOULD LIKE TO ASSURE YOU ALL THAT THIS IS AN OPEN FORUM. PLEASE SHARE YOUR OPINIONS FREELY.

3

*

This volume has a chapter focusing on our lovely Shibazaki.

I *love* drawing eyelashes. I had to *be* careful not to overdo it, though. Too many eyelashes make one's face look weird. I ended up erasing a lot of them. Girls just lighten up a whole page, don't you think? I'm committed to making them as pretty as I can. That's why the artwork on the cover has them surrounded by lots of flowers.

I take the responsibility seriously. The problem is... I *suck* at drawing flowers...

But that didn't stop me!

My heart desires to do the right thing. Am I just being naïve?
THE RAID IS COMING.
NO BULLETS. JUST OLD-FASHIONED HAND-TO-HAND COMBAT.
DON'T LET THEM LAY A FINGER ON IT.
LIBRARY TASK FORCE! GO!
SIR!

...TO PROTECT BOOKS, ALL BOOKS, WITH OUR LIVES!
WE'RE NOT HEROES.
I remember his words. I had just enlisted in the Library Forces.
MUNCH
MUNCH
BELLY'S FULL. ALL DONE.
I'M FULL JUST WATCHING YOU.
No organization is without its faults and compromises.
3 bowls...
THE BATCH IS COMING TODAY.
KICH
OFF I GO!
I know it in my heart.
But knowing doesn't make it any easier.
GOOD LUCK.

AS A JOURNALIST, SHE HAS HER REASONS.
HER ACTIONS ARE IN THE BEST INTEREST OF THE PUBLISHER.
DON'T JUDGE HER COMMITMENT TO HER WORK.
OUR COMMIT-MENT IS...

I FEEL LIKE SHE'S BETRAYED US.
PST
MISS ORIKUCHI.
I know she can be a hard-ass, but she has faith and she's not afraid to fight for it.
I admired that about her.
BLOCK-HEAD!
BONK

BEEP
BEEP
WE WILL DEFEND THE WEEKLY NEW WORLD!
THAT IS OUR DUTY!
IT'S YOUR MAGAZINE.
I'LL PROTECT IT WITH MY LIFE.

THE SENDER TRUSTED US WITH THIS MATERIAL.
I'LL BE DAMNED IF WE BURY IT LIKE A BUNCH OF SPINELESS APOLOGISTS.
BUT...
YOU DIDN'T HAVE TO PUT EVERYTHING OUT THERE LIKE THAT.
FOR SOME, IT'S JUST SENSATIONALISM EXPLOITING A TRAGEDY.
TURN
WE'RE PREPARED FOR IT.
IF IT'S NOT IN LINE WITH YOUR POLICY, WASH YOUR HANDS OF IT.
...HOW-EVER!

TELL ME...
WHAT IS IT YOU'RE TRYING TO ACCOMPLISH BY BREAKING THE LAW?
THAT DEPOSITION WAS SENT BY AN ANONYMOUS INSIDER.
MUST BE A CONCERNED PARTY UNHAPPY WITH THE RULING.
SOMEONE WANTED THE WORLD TO SEE IT...
...AND TO LET US DECIDE WHETHER THAT BOY DESERVED MORE THAN A SLAP ON THE WRIST.
The document shed light on the gruesome, gory details of the crimes.

It is a clear and flagrant violation of the juvenile court privacy laws.
SESOUSHA
WHAT'S GOING ON?
WHAT DO YOU MEAN?
YOU ALREADY KNOW "WHAT'S GOING ON."
WEEKLY NEW WORL EDITORIAL DEPARTMEN

HOW MUCH OF THE ARTICLE SHOULD WE RELEASE TO OUR PATRONS?
IT'S OUT OF OUR HANDS. WE'LL LEAVE IT TO THE LIBRARIANS.
The case's ruling caused a sensation. Many argued that the sentence was too light for someone who committed such atrocities.
It was fading from memory until the *Weekly New World* dropped a bombshell...
They acquired the court deposition in its entirety along with the perpetrator's image and full name.

WEEKLY NEW WOR
SPECIAL EDITION
Vol. 15
The controversy surrounds this issue.
It features an article on the teenage serial killer case that rocked the world last year.
WHAT'S GOING TO HAPPEN?
FIRST, A RAID.
THEY'LL MOST LIKELY AMBUSH WHEN THE BATCH IS DELIVERED TO THE LIBRARY. WE NEED TO TIGHTEN SECURITY.
AND THAT'S ONLY THE START OF OUR PROBLEMS.
3.

A well-rehearsed smile is useful!

CHAPTER 26

A well-rehearsed smile is useful!

WEEKLY NEW WORLD?
WHY...?!
THAT'S MISS ORIKUCHI'S MAGAZINE!
UNFORTUNATELY, IT *IS* TRUE.
...
THE OFFICIALS JUST CALLED.
THE LATEST ISSUE DUE OUT TOMORROW...
...WILL FEATURE AN ARTICLE THAT MAY VIOLATE THE LAW.
WEEKLY NE
NOT ONLY WILL IT BE A TARGET FOR CENSORSHIP...
...BUT IN THE MEANTIME WE HAVE TO DECIDE WHETHER OR NOT WE WILL ALLOW OUR PATRONS ACCESS TO IT.

After all these years, I found someone I actually want to be friends with.
IS IT TRUE...?

So why did I open up like that?
WILL YOU KEEP THIS BETWEEN US, KASAHARA?
As if...
...I had total faith in Kasahara, letting her see me be vulnerable.
You're *nothing*...
...like me.
It's not like me at all.

WHAT A FINE WAY TO START THE DAY...!
You're so honest, open...
...and lovable.
GRR! You keep doing this to me.
WHAT ?!
JUST PLEASE, GIVE IT A REST NOW AND THEN, YOU BLOCK-HEAD!
AW.
I'M SORRY, SIR.
I've never met any-one like you.

K'CHK
I'M GOING TO GO AND GET SECONDS!
BUMP
I WAS KIDDING. YOU HAVE NOTHING TO WORRY ABOUT.
BUT I'M NOT-
EEK!
Hi.
Mm.
You know...
Kasahara...
CLATTER

...
TH-
THAT'S YOUR CHOICE TO MAKE, SHIBA-ZAKI.
ARE YOU SURE?
SIP SIP
HOT
NONE OF MY BUSINESS!
YOU DON'T NEED MY PERMISSION.
Kasa-hara.

SIP
THAT'S THE KIND OF THING THAT MAKES HIM UNCOMFORT-ABLE.
Oh, dear.
YOU KNOW WHAT?
WHAT WOULD *YOU* DO IF I BECAME SERIOUS ABOUT OUR INSTRUCTOR DOJO?

I PROMISE. I WON'T BREATHE A WORD...
SNICKER
WHY ARE YOUR CHEEKS SUDDENLY HOLLOW?
WELL, JUST THE THOUGHT OF EVERYONE GANGING UP ON YOU...!
I sympa-thize...
HIROSE HAS ALWAYS BEEN A BUSYBODY.
THAT BLANK STARE DIDN'T FOOL ME. HE WAS DEFINITELY ALL EARS.
HEY. ARE YOU OKAY IF I TELL TEZUKA?
HEH HEH
NO PROBLEM WITH TEAM DOJO.
They're discreet.
Oh, by the way...
Would you tell Instructor Dojo that I'm a big fan?
I'm a pushover for cranky.
...

I hope Asahina shows up today. ♡
WHAT? HE WON'T COME EVERY DAY.
YOU NEVER KNOW. HE SEES A CHANCE AND GOES RIGHT FOR IT!
YAY!
IT'S NOT LIKE YOU THINK, HIROSE.
C'mon, don't be shy.
I THINK YOU TWO MAKE A CUTE COUPLE.
COME ON, HIROSE.
UH-OH.
Was it like that all day yesterday?
LATER, THEN.
YEP. EVERYONE WANTED A PIECE OF ME.
After Yesterday's Lunch
How did it go?
Did you say yes?
He's handsome!
YAY YAY
That was pretty much how you acted when I got back.
Eww. Sorry!

Even you, Kasahara.
CHIRP
CHIRP
CAFETE
GOOD MORNING, SHIBAZAKI, KASAHARA.
Morn-ing.
MORNING, HIROSE.
WHISPER
HEY. HEY.

Pay attention to details. Weasel your way in.
Manipulate information and people.
SNORK
If someone finds out about the *real* me, they'll think I'm despicable.
Okay. Time to sleep.
zzz
And yes...

My junior high school life sucked. I wouldn't repeat the same mistakes. I now had a network of friends to insulate me from social dangers.
YOU'VE GOT INCRED-IBLE PEOPLE SKILLS.
Every year, I got better at it.
REALLY?
I WISH I WAS LIKE YOU. WHAT'S THE KEY?
THERE'S NO KEY.
There is no way.
I don't get on with just anyone
Really?
No way I was going to tell her the truth.
The key to popu-larity is to never trust anyone.

UNBELIEV-ABLE.
SHE'S WICKED. WHY DO BOYS GO FOR HER?
SHE'S JUST A PRETTY FACE.
I chose a high school where I could avoid familiar faces.
From day one, I pre-tended to be kind.
Do you know his type...?
I hear he likes someone decent and kind.
I quickly made my way up to Miss Friendly, everyone's go-to girl.
LET'S HAVE LUNCH TOGETHER!
I kept my finger on the pulse of campus.
Winning popularity with sarcasm.
TEEHEEHEEHEE
What a sucker.
Harsh!

...THE OLDER BOY YOU HAVE A CRUSH ON?
BLUSH
WHY WOULD I GO OUT WITH SOMEONE I DON'T EVEN LIKE? WHO I DATE IS NONE OF YOUR BUSINESS.
SLAP
SLAP
YOU'RE HORRIBLE ...!
YOU'RE SO MEAN, SHIBAZAKI!
WAAAH
YOU HIT ME FIRST, REMEMBER?
BECAUSE ...
BECAUSE YOU SAID SOMETHING THAT BROKE MY HEART!

It's not like you, Asako Shibazaki.
THERE GOES SHIBAZAKI.
WHY IS SHE SO ARROGANT?
SHE'S JUST A PRETTY FACE.
HEY, THAT UPPER-CLASSMAN HAS GOT THE HOTS FOR SHIBAZAKI.
That's lame.
IS IT TRUE HE ASKED YOU OUT?
WHY DON'T YOU GO OUT WITH HIM?
He's a nice guy.
YOU MEAN...

NOT A WORD OF WHAT I SAID LEAVES THIS ROOM, OKAY?
WILL YOU KEEP THIS BETWEEN US, KASAHARA?
IF THE OTHER GIRLS HEAR ABOUT THIS, THEY'RE GOING TO BLOW IT OUT OF PROPOR-TION.
I PROMISE.
Why am I acting this way?
Want to take a bath?
Sounds nice.
I'm tired from being the butt of jokes.

I KNOW HOW YOU HATE TO BE THE SOURCE OF BAD NEWS.
GO GET HIM, SHIBAZAKI.
YAY♥
How funny.
I know it's not my business.
YOU DON'T LOOK ALL THAT EXCITED, SO...
For someone who's totally oblivious to all things in her own life...
Touché!
TICKLE TICKLE
WHOA
Stop!

He found a way in between my work and personal life. I couldn't say no.
Well.
He got me.
Me!
PST
YEAH, HE'S SMART, THOUGH I HATE TO ADMIT IT.
Here's...
...my card.
SO, ARE YOU GOING TO SEE HIM AGAIN?
IF OUR SCHED-ULES ALLOW, YES.
HE'S RESEARCHING LIBRARIES AND IS INTERESTED IN MY OPINIONS.
...
IF YOU DON'T WANT TO, JUST SAY SO.

How did it go?!
Well?!
...
PRETTY WELL, I GUESS.
I ACTUALLY HAD A BETTER TIME THAN I'D EXPECTED.
OH, REALLY?
THEN HE MUST BE PRETTY SMART, HUH? THIS GUY NAMED ASAHINA.
...
Actually... he *is*.
One minute a simpleton like Kasahara, the next keen and sharp.
Like what he said when we parted...
THERE'S NO ONE ELSE I KNOW AT THE LIBRARY.

WHAT?
THERE'S NO ONE ELSE I KNOW AT THE LIBRARY. MAY I PICK YOUR BRAIN NOW AND THEN?
WHEN IT'S NOT A BOTHER, OF COURSE.
I'M HOME.
WELCOME BACK!
GASP!

Someone like Kasahara.
DON'T YOU WORRY ABOUT IT.
Go ahead. Pry away.
...
THAT DOESN'T LOOK LIKE A PERFECTLY REHEARSED SMILE.
MUNCH MUNCH
EH?
NOTHING.
I'D LIKE TO TALK WITH YOU AGAIN, IF THAT'S OKAY.
Someone enjoys spying!
It's not like that.

I'M AFRAID THAT YOU'D HATE ME.
I DON'T MEAN TO PRY IF YOU'RE NOT COMFORTABLE WITH THIS KIND OF SUBJECT.
THE THING IS... WELL...
MUNCH MUNCH
GOD. WHAT AM I SAYING?
LET'S EAT.
SNICKER
AH HA HA HA!
MISS SHIBA-ZAKI?
Now there's a surprise.
EXCUSE ME.
CHUCKLE
So honest and direct! He reminds me of someone.

THE TERM HAS BEEN AROUND FOR A LONG TIME. I BELIEVE THERE WAS AN OCCURRENCE IN RECENT HISTORY, WASN'T THERE?
The incident happened at a library in Tokyo a few years ago.
Hundreds of books were secretly destroyed because of an MBC raid.
Apologist officials within the library were accused of letting the MBC have their way.
Modern day book burning.
YES.
I'M CURIOUS ABOUT YOUR FEELINGS...
...REGARDING THE *DARKER* SIDE OF THE LIBRARY'S HISTORY.
WHY WOULD YOU WANT *MY* OPINION...
A personal opinion?
Here's your order.
Ah.
WELL, I...
?

LATELY WE'RE DEALING WITH VARIOUS ISSUES SURROUNDING LIBRARIES.
LIKE... BOOK BURNING.
THAT'S A BIT...
... SERIOUS.
CLNK
Book burning.
The burning of controver-sial books to censor alternative view-points.

*

While I was working on this volume the world was going crazy for the 2010 World Cup!

Like everybody else, I was an enthusiastic fan even when I was at work. It was so exciting to watch the great matches on TV! Thanks to the teams for trying so hard!

Perhaps you can see my enthusiasm if you look at this volume's gag panels.

Sorry, I'm easily amused.

*

*

A guy like him can still be trouble.
WHAT ARE THEY SAYING?
IF YOU'RE SO ANXIOUS TO HEAR, WHY NOT SIT CLOSER TO THEIR TABLE?
What am I even doing here?
Kidnapped by Kasahara!
IDIOT! THAT'LL MAKE US GUILTY OF SPYING.
YOU WERE ALREADY GUILTY WHEN YOU DECIDED TO COME HERE.
WHAT IF HE TURNS OUT TO BE A WACKO?
I'M JUST A CONCERNED FRIEND.
WELL, HE SEEMS POLITE.
And... easy on the eyes!
Nuh-uh. There's a clear line between spying and accidentally overhearing, buddy.
Huh?
HOWEVER...
ha ha ha

YOUR MANNER IS SO KIND.
IT'S REALLY HELPFUL.
WELL, HAPPY TO BE OF SERVICE.
I DIDN'T EXPECT YOU TO ASK ME OUT, THOUGH.
OH.
I HATE TO TROUBLE YOU WHEN YOU'RE BUSY.
I JUST WANTED TO TALK TO YOU.
That infec-tious smile.
NO, NO TROUBLE AT ALL. WELL, EXCEPT FOR THE GOSSIPING COWORKERS BACK AT THE LIBRARY.
Sorry.
A nice young man indeed.
...
...
It seems he's just what he appears to be. Not bad-looking either.
But...

But *never* the way he did... declaring his intentions in front of everyone!
DING!
Welcome. I'll be right with you.
It's a lovely day, isn't it?
It'll just be the two of you?
Oops.
Tee hee!
Sorry.
SIGH
Pfft.
Well then.
It looks like word has made its way to other departments.
IN FACT, YOU'VE GIVEN ME GUIDANCE SEVERAL TIMES.

YOU COME TO THE LIBRARY QUITE OFTEN.
MR. ASAHINA, IF I'M NOT MISTAKEN?
THAT'S RIGHT! I'M HIKARU ASAHINA. I'M GLAD YOU REMEMBERED MY NAME.
I'm good with faces and names.
tee hee hee
Is that so?
ha ha ha
This is like a proper date.
I WAS WONDERING IF WE COULD HAVE LUNCH TOGETHER.
YES, SHE'D LOVE TO!
BUT I HAVE AN APPOINTMENT...
WITH KASAHARA, RIGHT? I'LL TELL HER YOU'RE BUSY.
GO.
...
SIP
It's not like this is the first time a guy has asked me out.

DO YOU KNOW WHO I AM, MISS SHIBAZAKI?
...
OF COURSE I DO.
What the...?
2.

CHAPTER 25

Secret admirer part 5

I WAS WONDERING IF WE COULD HAVE LUNCH TOGETHER.
...a fresh breeze comes blowing in.

REALLY?! BUT...
WHAT WAS TH-?
THAT WAS FOR KOMAKI. SHE ASKED ME TO HAND IT TO HIM BECAUSE HE WAS SO HARD TO CATCH.
...!
I see.
When the snow-flakes...
...are replaced by flower petals...
MISS SHIBA-ZAKI?
WHAT TIME IS YOUR LUNCH BREAK?

NEWS-FLASH.
THIS IS THE FIRST AND ONLY CHOCOLATE I GOT TODAY, YOU BLOCK-HEAD!
BOOF
CRUNCH MUNCH

CRUNCH

LET GO, SIR.
TUG TUG TUG
I DON'T THINK SO.
HUH?
I WANT TO EAT IT.
WHAT...?!
Did you hear what I said?!
SWING
I'M EXHAUSTED FROM FIXING YOUR SCREW-UPS. I COULD USE A SUGAR FIX.
Let go.
B-BUT...
Not gonna let go!
I SAW SOMEONE GIVING YOU CHOCOLATE. CHOCOLATE THAT'S MUCH PRETTIER.

WHAT IS THIS?
GAH!
CHO
NOOOOO!
CLAMP
CRINGE
ZSH ZSH ZSH
THAT'S... WELL... UMM...
The way you move is truly frightening.
IT'S TOO CHEAP.
NOTHING.
YOU WON'T LIKE IT, SIR.

IT'S...
...SNOWING.
WOW
IT'S SNOWING!
IT'S CERTAINLY COLD ENOUGH TO SNOW.
WHEEE
ROLL ROLL
THE FIRST SNOW OF THE WINTER!
YOU'LL CATCH A COLD, YOU BLOCK-HEAD.
BOFF
CHOCO

...after he got that beautifully wrapped chocolate?
NO.
NOTHING, SIR.
K'CHK
WHAT'S WITH YOU TODAY?

OH!
CHOCO MINT
Already opened...
I put it in my pocket and forgot about it.
RIP...
YOU DON'T WANT IT? FINE. MORE FOR ME.
WAIT UP!
Now's your chance. Give it to him...!
WHAT?
You're going to give this...
UM...

LET'S GET IT FINISHED SO WE CAN GO HOME!
BEEP
21:15
I'M SO SORRY ABOUT TODAY.
SIGH
DON'T BE.
YOU STINK AT DETAIL-ORIENTED TASKS. I'M NOT SURPRISED.
GRR!
Yes.
SIR.
RUSTLE
WHAT'S THIS?

KASAHARA....
Yes?
LOOK AT THE FILE! IT'S OFF BY A ROW FROM PAGE TWO TO THE END!
!
Hard copy
REDO
EEK!
YOU BLOCK-HEAD!
OVERTIME
Deskwork is...
...not her forte.
I'LL FIX IT RIGHT AWAY.
GIVE ME HALF. I'LL LEND YOU A HAND.
HUH?

CLICK
EMPTY
...
I didn't have a chance to stock up.
"Hey, Dojo." Hmm...
GLANCE
Perhaps they enlisted at the same time...
I'M FINISHED ENTERING DATA.
19:18
OKAY.

...INSTRUCTOR DOJO HAS HIS OWN LITTLE FOLLOWING.
Today is Valentine's Day.
It's homemade.
A day when girls give chocolate to the ones they love.

What?
Why am I hiding?
MAYBE...
THMP THMP

I'm not giving up until Instructor Dojo gets...
OH.
SIR-
HEY, DOJO?
SHP

OH, DEAR. WHAT DO THEY SEE IN THIS STIFF?
RIGHT BACK AT YOU.
Who wants to date a sarcastic shrew?
IF YOU HAVEN'T HAD LUNCH YET...
CARE TO JOIN ME?
?!
WHAT ?!
I JUST WANT TO SCARE THEM OFF WHILE I EAT.
Work with me, stiff.
LET'S CIRCLE THE WAGONS.
It's freezing out here. Have you got a hand-warmer?
Nope.
SHF
I want her chocolate...
SHF
Tezuka...
TMP
THE CHIEF'S SUCH A BIG PIG!
TMP
TMP
It's all right. I'll just go and buy more.

WOULD YOU ACCEPT MY ...?
SORRY. CAN'T.
IF YOU DON'T ALREADY HAVE SOMEONE SPECIAL...
...WOULD YOU LIKE TO GO OUT WITH M-
I'M SORRY.
SOB SOB
OH?
HMM?
SOB SOB
ANOTHER HEART BROKEN, ROMEO?
THAT'S RICH, COMING FROM *YOU*.

WEEKLY NEW
TCH TCH
...
FROM
Maki Origuchi
TO
Ryusuke Genda
SHE ACTS LIKE A SCHOOLGIRL SOMETIMES.
UM...
TEZUKA.
ERM...
MISS SHIBA-ZAKI...

Hello.
I'm Kiiro Yumi.
This is the sixth volume of *Library Wars*.

I know I keep saying it, but I never get used to it.
Oh my god!
My sixth book is in bookstores!

I feel so grateful to be a part of this.
I am thankful to everyone involved.

Thank you so much!

Hope you enjoy it from cover to cover!

Morning.
DOJO JUST CALLED. HE'LL BE IN AFTER LUNCH.
Huh?!
?!
THE GUY WHO SAT NEXT TO HIM AT YESTERDAY'S MEETING HAD THE FLU.
Oh no!
WHAT HAPPENED? IS HE ALL RIGHT?
DOJO FEELS FINE, BUT NO HARM IN GETTING A CHECK-UP.
Saves us from having to do the same.
Is this from you, Kasahara?
I'll have one.
GLANCE
Will there be enough to go around? Looks like it.
'Sup.
CHOCO-LATE?

YOU DON'T WANT IT? FINE. MORE FOR ME.
RIP...
VWOOSH
PLAIN CHOCOLATE, BUT CHOCOLATE FROM A GIRL NONETHELESS!
CHOCO MINI
Good.
That's it for this year.
Oh?
Will it be the same next year?
Nevermind!
This is the simplest way to make sure Instructor Dojo gets some chocolate.
Got one.
Obligatory.
I'll have one then.
One for me.
...
What have we here?
CLENCH

It's up to me to give the brute courtesy chocolate!
SWEET
14 1 2
COURTESY CHOCOLATE FOR EVERYONE ON THE TASK FORCE.
HELP YOURSELVES, GENTLEMEN!
TA DA!
CHOCO MINI
HUH.
Kasahara! Isn't this a little impersonal even for courtesy chocolate?
I'M THE ONLY GIRL ON THE FORCE. I CAN'T POSSIBLY COVER EVERYONE.

TEAM DOJO WILL HAVE A BUSY DAY.
INSTRUCTOR KOMAKI AND TEZUKA HAVE LOTS OF FANS.
MAYBE INSTRUCTOR DOJO HAS HIS OWN LITTLE FOLLOWING.
BWAH HAH!
WHAT, HIM?
KASA-HARA.
DON'T MAKE THAT FACE.
Appalling.
BWA HA HA HA HA HA HA HA HA!
THAT BRUTE? NO WAY.
...
You're kidding yourself.
Did you catch a cold?
Drinking in Dojo's room
No way that's going to happen.
It's cold.
Let's hurry back to the room.
Poor bastard.

Who would I give chocolate to anyway?
Deskwork starts today.
You'll be out of your comfort zone. Keep on your toes!
GOT ANY PLANS FOR VALENTINE'S DAY, SHIBAZAKI?
SPLOOSH
GIRLS IN MY DEPARTMENT GIVE SWEETS TO EVERYONE AS A GROUP TO PRESERVE ANONYMITY.
SO, NO. NO PLANS.
Think about it. If a knockout like me plays favorites there will be blood in the streets.
I'd make an exception for Instructor Dojo though.♡
...
How kind.

...IF I COULD ONLY FIND MY PRINCE.
WHAT A FINE WAY TO START THE DAY!
YOU'RE THINKING OUT LOUD AGAIN.
INSTRUCTOR DOJO!
You sneak up like a thief!
I'm not a thief!
HURRY INTO THE BUILDING. THE MEETING STARTS SOON.
YES, SIR.
That's right.
There's no one.

NO, DUMMY.
DO YOU REALIZE WHAT MONTH THIS IS?
SUN
2
2020
SHOKA 32
HUH...?
OH.
Morning!
BRRR
Valentine's Day. Hmm.
That's why the girls are all giggling about chocolate and boys.
...
I'D JOIN THE FUN...

WHO'S FILLING HIS SHOES?
I hope it's someone more fit for the position.
IT'S STILL VERY HUSH-HUSH.
We can't allow another incident like that.
Oh!
SPEAKING OF INSTRUCTOR KOMAKI, MARIE WAS AT THE LIBRARY TODAY.
Yeah.
I SAW HER TOO!
She's started using her real voice with us.
Speech is a struggle for Marie as she can't control her volume.
She's totally opening up to us. ♡
Is that cute or what?!
THIS IS A SPECIAL MONTH FOR US...!
SIP
THAT'S WHAT MARIE SAID. IS KOMAKI'S BIRTHDAY THIS MONTH OR SOMETHING?

NO SNOW YET FOR TOKYO
KI RESORTS STAY CLOSED
RUMOR HAS IT THAT ACTING DIRECTOR TOBA WILL BE REASSIGNED.
REALLY?
HE'S BEING HELD RESPONSIBLE FOR THE ABDUCTION OF INSTRUCTOR KOMAKI LAST MONTH.
It was generous of the commander to wait until the end of his term.
...I CAN AUTHORIZE THE REMOVAL OF MIKIHISA KOMAKI BY THE MEDIA BETTERMENT COMMITTEE.
HMM.
Long overdue...!

1.
PK Showdown

library wars
Love & War
CHAPTER 24

library wars
Love & War

The Library Freedom Act

Libraries have the freedom to acquire their collections.

Libraries have the freedom to circulate materials in their collections.

Libraries guarantee the privacy of their patrons.

Libraries oppose any type of censorship.

When libraries are imperiled,
librarians will join together
to secure their freedom.

Library Wars

Love & War

Contents

Library Wars

6

Love & War

STORY & ART BY Kiiro Yumi ORIGINAL CONCEPT BY Hiro Arikawa